# the divine deal

## Student Work Book

Sherry Matthews Plaster

# the divine deal

## Student Work Book

Sherry Matthews Plaster

WWW.SHERRYMATTHEWSPLASTER.COM

# The Divine Deal Student Work Book

© 2017 by Sherry Matthews Plaster

All rights reserved

ISBN:0692965610
eISBN:

*This Guide is designed to help you on your journey through The Divine Deal and truly help you to discover and understand God's wonderful plan for your life*

# CONTENTS

INTRODUCTION · 9

CHAPTER ONE
    LOVE IS THE KEY · 11

CHAPTER TWO
    WHO ARE YOU? · 15

CHAPTER THREE
    IT'S TIME TO TALK · 21

CHAPTER FOUR
    RESISTING TEMPTATION: IT'S YOUR CHOICE · 27

CHAPTER FIVE
    BELEIVING IS SEEING · 33

CHAPTER SIX
    TWO KINDS OF FEAR · 39

CHAPTER SEVEN
    DO YOUR BEST · 45

CHAPTER EIGHT
    TWO KINDS OF ANGER · 49

CHAPTER NINE
    FORGIVE EVERYTHING? · 55

CHAPTER TEN
    YOUR GREATEST FANS                                              61

CHAPTER ELEVEN
    LOVING OTHERS                                                      67

CHAPTER TWELVE
    NO ROOM FOR ENVY                                             73

CHAPTER THIRTEEN
    HOW SERIOUS IS GOSSIP?                                  79

CHAPTER FOURTEEN
    HOW ABOUT A LITTLE WHITE LIE?                  83

# INTRODUCTION
# THE DIVINE DEAL

SUMMARY:

Your life is your own and God has a divine plan for you. It's important to allow God to take control of the wheel and guide you. And if this is not done, the consequences are lasting and at times irreversible.

POINTS TO REMEMBER:

- ❖ YOUR LIFE IS YOURS. No-one else can live it for you.
- ❖ As you prepare for your life as an adult, you will face many crucial decisions that will
- ❖ greatly influence the rest of your life, BE WISE.
- ❖ There are consequences for each decision.
- ❖ God is love, and He loves YOU and has a divine plan for your life.
- ❖ Understand that life without God is like trying to nail gelatin to the wall.

DO YOU HAVE ANY QUESTIONS? WRITE THEM HERE:

........................................................................................................................

........................................................................................................................

........................................................................................................................

........................................................................................................................

........................................................................................................................

........................................................................................................................

........................................................................................................................

........................................................................................................................

SCRIPTURE VERSES TO MEMORIZE:

> "For I know the thoughts that I think toward you, says the Lord, thoughts of peace and not of evil, to give you a future and a hope."
> ~ Jeremiah 29:11

**Closing and Prayer:** *Lord Jesus help us to realize to its fullest measure that you have a great plan for our lives. Constantly remind me how much you love me, open my eyes to this. I don't want to go through life without your guidance God, I want to honor you in all that I do. Amen.*

# CHAPTER ONE
## LOVE IS THE KEY

SCRIPTURE:

*Jesus replied: "Love the Lord your God with all your heart and with all your soul and with all your mind. This is the first and greatest commandment. And the second is like it: Love your neighbor as yourself. All the law and the prophets hang on these two commandments."*
~ Matthew 22:37–40

SUMMARY:

The first chapter sets the tone for the entire book. It outlines right away that, as humans, love is our greatest need. God instructs us that the greatest commandment is to love Him first, and then love others second. Without love, and others to love, our lives are meaningless. The focus of success or failure in our lives will be measured by the difference we made in other people's lives, through our loving actions. In order to truly love others, and show them the love of Christ, we first need to love God. Not only should we love God, but we should be in love with God. To have an intimate relationship with Christ means that He comes first in our lives, that we hold a desire to be more like him. We need to think with a Christ-like mindset in order to act with Christ-like behavior. Then, and only then, if we have this Christ-like mindset will we be able to grasp what it is like to love like Christ. God's commandments to love are not to keep us in bondage, but to free us from bondage, and to live a freedom filled life. These commandments will not only guide us to make good decisions, but also will bring us closer in our relationship with Christ. The only way to live a successful life is if we put Christ and His commandments at the center of our lives.

POINTS TO REMEMBER:

- ❖ LOVE IS OUR GREATEST HUMAN need
- ❖ Success today and in the future is determined by whom we choose to love and honor
- ❖ God's instructions are clear: first and most important, honor Him in love. Second, we are to honor others in love just as we love ourselves.

QUESTION & ANSWER SESSION:

*End of Chapter Questions to Consider:*

- ❖ Have you committed yourself to learning to live as God intends?
- ❖ Would you rather fit in with others, or be set apart living a successful life?
- ❖ Are you ready to forsake foolishness in your life?
- ❖ What changes do you need to make in your life today regarding obedience?

DO YOU HAVE ANY QUESTIONS? WRITE THEM HERE:

................................................................................................

................................................................................................

................................................................................................

................................................................................................

................................................................................................

................................................................................................

................................................................................................

................................................................................................

SCRIPTURE VERSES TO MEMORIZE:

*Jesus replied: "Love the Lord your God with all your heart and with all your soul and with all your mind. This is the first and greatest commandment. And the second is like it: Love your neighbor as yourself. All the law and the prophets hang on these two commandments."*
~ Matthew 22:37–40

*God is love. Whoever lives in love lives in God, and God in him. In this way, love is made complete among us so that we will have confidence on the day of judgment, because in this world we are like him.*
~ 1 John 4:16–17

JOURNAL YOUR THOUGHTS, WHAT DID YOU GAIN AND LEARN FROM THIS STUDY:

..................................................................................................................

..................................................................................................................

..................................................................................................................

..................................................................................................................

..................................................................................................................

..................................................................................................................

..................................................................................................................

..................................................................................................................

**Closing and Prayer:** *Lord, We want to thank You for loving us first, so that we can also love. Thank You for taking time to get to know us, and loving us in the ways we each specifically need. Lord, remind us that Your love is the greatest love, and it's the only love we need to rely on. Teach us to love others like You love us, give us the capacity to do so. We love You Lord, and we are so grateful for Your loving kindness. Amen.*

# CHAPTER TWO
## WHO ARE YOU?

SCRIPTURE:

> *"You did not choose me, but I chose you and appointed you to go and bear fruit—fruit that will last. Then the Father will give you what- ever you ask in my name."*
>
> ~ John 15:16

SUMMARY:

The second chapter details the importance of finding who you are in Gods eyes. An emphasis is put on how superior humans are compared to the rest of God's creation. As humans, we were chosen by God, with a specific design, and a specific plan for our lives. Before He formed us in the womb, we were already set apart, appointed to be a disciple for him. Our lives hold purpose and meaning, because of his divine plan for our lives. We are to be the salt of the earth and the light of the world, set apart from those of the world. We are to show the beauty of God's love within us, as that was a part of His purpose in creating us. You may deal with insecurities, feelings of self-doubt or self-hatred, but there is a God who specifically designed you the way you are, One who can turn your insecurities into securities, and your self-doubt into strength.

Outward beauty is fleeting, people love you because of what is inward, as you do the same for others. God looks at the character of our hearts, not our outward appearance. Even though we have confidence through

Christ, the bible also instructs us to treat our bodies as temples. This includes keeping our food intake appropriate, not to be over indulgent in anything, which includes eating and drinking. God made you special- your circumstances do not define you, only your relationship with Christ does. Regardless of where you come from, what family you are in, regardless of the class in which society has you placed, in God's eyes, we are all the same when it comes to social structure. He made YOU with purpose, He has a specific plan for you and you only. This should challenge you to be the best version of yourself that you can be.

POINTS TO REMEMBER:

- ❖ YOU are superior to all of God's creation because your life is purposeful.

- ❖ YOU are unique by design, chosen by God. Because you were chosen by God, you must know that He has a divine and specific plan for your life.

- ❖ YOUR life has purpose and meaning.

- ❖ Outward beauty does not compare to the inward content of your heart and soul. God cares about what is on the inside, not your outward appearance.

- ❖ Do not let anything stop you from achieving your dreams, God had instilled passions in you for a purpose.

QUESTION & ANSWER:

*End of Chapter Questions to Consider:*

- ❖ How does your self-image line up with who God says you are?
- ❖ God's Word vs. people: When they conflict, which do you believe?
- ❖ What are some of your gifts, and what do you intend to do with them?

*End of Chapter Questions to Consider and to Research:*

- ❖ Who is Oprah Winfrey?
- ❖ What socioeconomic class did she come from?
- ❖ What happened to her in her youth, and how did she overcome it?

DO YOU HAVE ANY QUESTIONS? WRITE THEM HERE:

...........................................................................................................................

...........................................................................................................................

...........................................................................................................................

...........................................................................................................................

...........................................................................................................................

...........................................................................................................................

...........................................................................................................................

...........................................................................................................................

SCRIPTURE VERSES TO MEMORIZE:

*"Before I formed you in the womb I knew you, before you were born I set you apart;*
*I appointed you as a prophet to the nations."*

~ Jeremiah 1:5

*"For you created my inmost being; you knit me together in my mother's womb.*
*I praise you because I am fearfully and wonderfully made; your works are wonderful, I know that full well."*

~ Psalm 139:13–14

JOURNAL YOUR THOUGHTS, WHAT DID YOU GAIN AND LEARN FROM THIS STUDY:

..................................................................................................................

..................................................................................................................

..................................................................................................................

..................................................................................................................

..................................................................................................................

..................................................................................................................

..................................................................................................................

..................................................................................................................

..................................................................................................................

**Closing and Prayer:** *Lord, I just want to thank you. I thank you for creating me, I thank you for forming me, setting me apart before you even knew me. I want to thank you for making me feel special when nothing else does. Thank you for guiding me, walking ahead of me in life, making a way for me. Thank you Lord for constantly reminding me how beautiful I am to you. That I don't have to rely on the opinions of others, that I should only be concerned about Yours. Thank you Lord for giving me a personal relationship with you that makes me secure in who I am, and our relationship. Amen.*

# CHAPTER THREE
# IT'S TIME TO TALK

SCRIPTURE:

*"Then you will call upon Me and come pray to Me, and I will listen to you. You will seek Me and find Me when you seek Me with all your heart."*

~ Jeremiah 29:12-13

SUMMARY:

Talking to God is crucial for our relationship with God to grow. Think about your relationship with your best friend, and how much communication is involved. Do you communicate with God as frequently as you do with your best friend? Often times people think that if their prayers are not answered then God is not listening. That is not true, sometimes God's answer is simply no or to wait. We are instructed to pray continually, in all things, which will strengthen our relationship with Christ. God is always listening; it is upon us to talk to Him. Not only are we told to pray continually but we are to give thanks continually. If we are continuously praying and giving thanks, then our minds will be set on Him. If our minds are set on Jesus then we will have a more positive outlook, turning our mind and attitude in a more positive direction. We are to be persistent in our prayer life, regardless of the circumstances. We are to remember that God is sovereign. We are to approach God with confidence but in respect. Not only should we lift up our prayer requests to God, but those of others.

Pray for your family, pray for your friends, pray for those who serve the country, pray for those in need. God will answer your prayers in His time and in His way. Pray for God to bring direction in your life, pray for Him to lead you in the path of His perfect will.

POINTS TO REMEMBER:

- ❖ Four main points to remember regarding prayer:
    1. God hears ALL your prayers.
    2. He answers ALL your prayers.
    3. He answers prayer in His time, not yours.
    4. Sometimes His answer will be no.
- ❖ Your prayer life is crucial in order to become more intimate in your relationship with Christ.
- ❖ God might not always answer your prayer the way you wanted, He might even say no.
- ❖ Pray continually, and give thanks always.
- ❖ Regardless of our circumstances, God is sovereign.
- ❖ Ask for guidance in all things, and wait for Gods answer.
- ❖ Follow His lead, for then you will never fail.

QUESTION & ANSWER:

*End of Chapter Questions to Consider:*

- ❖ What are some of the benefits of prayer?
- ❖ How often does God hear from you? Does He hear from you enough?
- ❖ Do you ask and then wait for God's direction in decision making?
- ❖ Do you remember to pray for others?

DO YOU HAVE ANY QUESTIONS? WRITE THEM HERE:

........................................................................................................................

........................................................................................................................

........................................................................................................................

........................................................................................................................

........................................................................................................................

........................................................................................................................

........................................................................................................................

........................................................................................................................

........................................................................................................................

........................................................................................................................

SCRIPTURE VERSES TO MEMORIZE:

*"Be joyful always; pray continually, give thanks in all circumstances, for this is God's will for you in Christ Jesus."*
~ 1 Thessalonians 5:16–18

*"And the Lord said, "Listen to what the unjust judge says. And will not God bring about justice for His chosen ones, who cry out to Him day and night? Will He keep putting them off? I tell you, He will see that they get justice, and quickly."*
~ Luke 18:6–8

JOURNAL YOUR THOUGHTS, WHAT DID YOU GAIN AND LEARN FROM THIS STUDY:

..................................................................................................

..................................................................................................

..................................................................................................

..................................................................................................

..................................................................................................

..................................................................................................

..................................................................................................

..................................................................................................

**Closing and Prayer:** *Dear Lord, Thank You for letting me talk to you so freely. Thank you for giving me the ability and the freedom to come to You in complete honesty and rawness. Lord, I know You know the desires of my heart before I voice them. I know You know my greatest struggles and my greatest weaknesses before I bring them to You. Thank You for preparing my way before I even ask. Thank You for always being there to listen no matter the time of day, or the type of prayer. Thank You for not leaving my side when I get angry at You, Lord. Thank You for being gracious, Amen.*

# CHAPTER FOUR
## RESISTING TEMPTATION: IT'S YOUR CHOICE

SCRIPTURE:

*"When tempted, no one should say, "God is tempting me." For God cannot be tempted by evil, nor does He tempt anyone; but each one is tempted when, by his own desire, he is dragged away and enticed."*

~ James 1:13–14

SUMMARY:

Temptation is a scary word. It is a part of everyday life, a struggle that we all must face. When temptation strikes, you will ultimately find that doing the right thing is more rewarding than doing the wrong alternative. Temptation is all around us, evil desires come from within due to our sinful nature. Satan will use enticing things and enticing people to tempt you to fall under pressure. Satan temps us to live in the moment, to hold no regard for repercussions that will follow sinful actions. In order to overcome these temptations, we must put all of our faith in God and fully trust Him that He will help you overcome the temptations. God will not tempt us, but He will test us. The entire book of Job is dedicated to lessons on strength and faith. Satan wanted to test Jobs strength, he believed with enough trials Job would curse God. Job experienced so much heartache, death, and disease. However, Job remained faithful to God, and was blessed. Job taught us that no matter the level of your faithfulness, there will still be suffering in your life. Not only did God allow Satan to tempt

Job, but He allowed His own son to be tempted as well. The Spirit led Jesus into the desert where He fasted for forty days and forty nights. Exhausted, and starving, Satan appeared to Jesus. He tried to tempt Him, in multiple ways, but he found His strength in His Father. We need to follow Christ's lead and find our strength in God when temptations come along. The Lord will instantly help us; He is there waiting for us to look to Him for help. We all struggle with different temptations. Learn to keep yourself from those situations, and learn to leave when it's needed. Every time you resist temptation you are becoming more like Jesus. You will become stronger and wiser, but never lose sight of the One who gives you strength.

POINTS TO REMEMBER:

- ❖ We are human, our nature is sinful, so temptations will rise from within us. Through God's strength we are able to resist those temptations and do what is right, and will be rewarded in the end.

- ❖ Nothing will come into your life that God can't bring you through, He will provide a way out of every temptation as long as you focus on Him and allow Him to be your strength.

- ❖ Sometimes we must experience negative circumstances to grow in our faith, like Job did.

- ❖ Follow Jesus' lead and find your strength in the Lord when things get tough.

- ❖ Each event in life is a learning experience, if you chose to seek God first in all things, then you will learn the easier way.

- ❖ Temptation is not a sin, but giving into it is. Walk circumspectly.

QUESTION & ANSWER:

*End of Chapter Questions to Consider:*

- ❖ How do you deal with temptation?
- ❖ Do you need to change the way you deal with temptation?
- ❖ Do you often deal with the same temptation?

*End of Chapter Questions to Research:*

- ❖ What did Jesus' disciple Judas do when tempted to deny Him?
- ❖ What happened because of his decision?

DO YOU HAVE ANY QUESTIONS? WRITE THEM HERE:

..................................................................................................................................

..................................................................................................................................

..................................................................................................................................

..................................................................................................................................

..................................................................................................................................

..................................................................................................................................

..................................................................................................................................

..................................................................................................................................

..................................................................................................................................

SCRIPTURE VERSES TO MEMORIZE:

*"Submit yourselves, then, to God. Resist the devil and he will flee from you."*

~ James 4:7

*"It is written: 'Man does not live by bread alone, but on every word that comes from the mouth of God.'"*

~ Matthew 4:4

JOURNAL YOUR THOUGHTS, WHAT DID YOU GAIN AND LEARN FROM THIS STUDY:

........................................................................................................

........................................................................................................

........................................................................................................

........................................................................................................

........................................................................................................

........................................................................................................

........................................................................................................

........................................................................................................

........................................................................................................

........................................................................................................

**Closing and Prayer:** *Lord, thank You for providing me with the strength I need to get through each day. I could not get through a single day without You by my side, Lord. Continue to remind me that Your strength is greater than my own, that there is no need to lean on my own understanding when I have You. Thank you for giving me the strength to resist the temptations that are placed in my path each day. Lord, I will continue to try to seek You first in all situations, but I need Your help and Your guidance to stay faithful with this. Temptation is scary, Lord, but I know you're stronger than all the temptations of the world put together as one. There is no need to be fearful when You are on my side God. Amen.*

# CHAPTER FIVE
# BELEIVING IS SEEING

SCRIPTURE:

*"And without faith it is impossible to please God, because anyone who comes to Him must believe that He exists and that He rewards those who earnestly seek Him."*

Hebrews 11:6

SUMMARY:

In chapter five, the topic of faith is discussed. Having faith isn't simply believing in God, but also the promises and the instructions written in His word. Having faith is believing that God is all powerful and that He will do what He has promised in His word. In order to grow in our faith, we must study the bible. By studying the bible, we will grow closer to Christ in our relationship with Him. Through our faith, we will strive to obey Him and to please Him. Faith not only teaches us of God's grace, but of His wrath as well. We learn about the power He has and His ability to use it. It is a given that we will face hardships throughout our lives, and it is our choice whether or not we turn to Christ or away from Christ. Christ wants us to pull close to Him, not away from Him, He is there to be our strength, our refuge. Be like Job, turn to God in faith, unwavering faith, and stay in constant prayer. Because of Job's faith, God blessed him with double to that which he had. When God is in control of your life, you will be able to feel his strength guiding you through things. Another faithful man of God was Noah, he loved God while living in the midst of so many wicked people. Noah kept his faith, and God favored him and his family. Noah faced immense ridicule for his faith in the Lord, while he worked for 120 years on an ark that people thought he was insane for building. God kept His promises to Noah and destroyed all but the Ark in the flood. It's very important to listen to and confirm what the Lord is telling you for He may bring you in a direction that you did not anticipate at all. How do we anticipate this? By asking, praying, and having faith in Him and then LISTENING and expecting and watching for His answer. The right doors will open and the wrong doors will close.

POINTS TO REMEMBER:

- ❖ Faith is not only believing in a one, sovereign God, but also believing the instructions and promises in His word to be true.

- ❖ Faith is not only believing that there is one ultimate supreme God but also believing all the instructions and promises in His Word are for you.

- ❖ Studying Gods word draws us closer to Him.

- ❖ During hard times when so many Christians turn away from God rather than clinging to Him. Make a decision to cling to Christ and the love and strength He provides for us.

- ❖ When you need God the most, turn to Him and not away from Him.

- ❖ Dwell in the consolation of God's truth, all trials will pass.

- ❖ Stay steadfast in your faith, and strive to seek the path God has for you by earnestly seeking Him in prayer for that guidance. He will show you His will when you seek Him with all your heart.

- ❖ The apostle Paul said our faith should never rest on the wisdom of others but in and on God's power.

- ❖ Don't ever concern yourself with what others may think of you, what you're doing, or what you're trying to do; Noah didn't, David didn't, and Judge Benjamin didn't either.

- ❖ Ask, pray, seek, have faith in Him and His perfect ways.

QUESTION & ANSWER:

*End of Chapter Questions to Consider:*

- ❖ Where are you in your faith?
- ❖ Do you have faith in God's promises for your life?
- ❖ Are you willing to step out in faith and do whatever God leads you to do?
- ❖ Do you worry more about what people think or what God thinks of you?

DO YOU HAVE ANY QUESTIONS? WRITE THEM HERE:

............................................................................................................................................

............................................................................................................................................

............................................................................................................................................

............................................................................................................................................

............................................................................................................................................

SCRIPTURE VERSES TO MEMORIZE:

*"A righteous man may have many troubles, but the Lord delivers him from them all."*

~ Psalm 34:19

*"We live by faith, not by sight."*

~ 2 Corinthians 5:7

JOURNAL YOUR THOUGHTS, WHAT DID YOU GAIN AND LEARN FROM THIS STUDY:

...............................................................................................................

...............................................................................................................

...............................................................................................................

...............................................................................................................

...............................................................................................................

...............................................................................................................

...............................................................................................................

...............................................................................................................

...............................................................................................................

...............................................................................................................

...............................................................................................................

**Closing and Prayer:** *Dear Lord, Thank You for providing us with the bible so that we may have a clear outline of your instructions for us. Not only does it provide us with guidelines, but it provides us with all of Your promises for us. We are blessed, Lord, because You provide us, so abundantly, with promises, that we are so undeserving of. Lord, guide me in my biblical studies, draw me in closer to You as we walk through scripture, and in prayer, together. Lord, remind me to turn to You in all situations, not just the bad, not just the good, but ALL situations. It is so important for me to keep this in the front of my mind. Lord I will ask, pray, seek, and have faith in You and Your perfect ways in all situations. Thank You Lord, Amen.*

# CHAPTER SIX
## TWO KINDS OF FEAR

SCRIPTURE:

*"But blessed is the man who trusts in the Lord, whose confidence is in Him. He will be like a tree planted by the water that sends out its roots by the stream. It does not fear when heat comes; its leaves are always green. It has no worries in a year of drought and never fails to bear fruit."*

~ Jeremiah 17:7–8

SUMMARY:

Fear is a common feeling that all people struggle with. There are two main types of fear. There is the emotion of fear and the spirit of fear. The emotion of fear is natural, as God gave us emotions, but the spirit of fear comes from the devil. Like temptation, the devil uses fear to cripple and control us. A spirit of fear does not come from the Lord, if we live by faith, then we have absolutely nothing to fear. God calls us to have a 'sound mind' and through Him to be disciplined in our ways. We need to use the strength that comes from the Holy Spirit in order to counter the spirit of fear that comes from the devil. The three most common fears include the fear of failure, the fear of rejection, and the fear that God will not provide for our needs. God sets passions and desires in our hearts for specific reason. The fear of failure will creep in and tell us we are not good enough to do these things. The fear of failure can keep us from trusting

God with our passions and can cause us to miss out on great things. The fear of rejection is also detrimental as it can hinder you from fully loving others the way God intended for you to do so. We are God's children, and He promises to take care of all of His children. His promises are clear, He will provide for us. Even though Job had faith in God, he still feared that God would not provide for his needs. Allowing fear to enter into your mind will allow the devil to have a foothold into your soul. We are the Lord's chosen ones, who will accomplish great things, so we should not fear anything but the Lord Himself. Although it is impossible to fathom the greatness of God's power, the small amount that we can should also instill fear and reverence in our hearts as well. If we fear His wrath then we will try to keep His commandments. Fear, naturally, will cause us to heed something due to the repercussions of partaking in something. This applies to our fear with God as well, because we know of His wrath for those that disobey, so it steers us away from disobeying Him. We should fear the Lord, but not Satan, as he is no threat to us if God is in us. Our faith should cause us to fear not, knowing God is in control of all things.

POINTS TO REMEMBER:

- ❖ Fear is the most common struggle that is brought as a temptation from the devil.

- ❖ Hold on to God's promises and keep steadfast in your faith and you will have nothing to fear.

- ❖ The three most common fears include the fear of failure, the fear of rejection, and the fear that God will not provide for our needs.

- ❖ Do not let the fear of failure cause you to miss out on the passions that God instilled in your heart.

- ❖ Do not let the fear of rejection hinder you from loving others to your full potential.

- ❖ Do not let the fear that God will not provide, cause you to stumble in your relationship with Christ. God will provide as He has promised.

- ❖ Love the Lord with your whole heart, but also fear Him with your whole heart.

- ❖ If we fear His wrath, then we will try to keep his commandments.

- ❖ If you have faith in God, there is nothing you should fear except for God himself.

QUESTION & ANSWER:

*End of Chapter Questions to Consider:*

- ❖ What are some of your fears?
- ❖ Do you have within you the spirit of fear?
- ❖ How could the spirit of fear prevent you from achieving success in life?
- ❖ Do you fear God? Why?

DO YOU HAVE ANY QUESTIONS? WRITE THEM HERE:

..................................................................................................................

..................................................................................................................

..................................................................................................................

..................................................................................................................

..................................................................................................................

SCRIPTURE VERSES TO MEMORIZE:

*"There is no fear in love. But perfect love drives out fear, because fear has to do with punishment. The one who fears is not made perfect in love."*

~ 1 John 4:18

*"Do not be afraid of those who kill the body but cannot kill the soul. Rather, be afraid of the One who can destroy both the soul and body in hell."*

~ Matthew 10:28

JOURNAL YOUR THOUGHTS, WHAT DID YOU GAIN AND LEARN FROM THIS STUDY:

...........................................................................................................................

...........................................................................................................................

...........................................................................................................................

...........................................................................................................................

...........................................................................................................................

...........................................................................................................................

...........................................................................................................................

...........................................................................................................................

...........................................................................................................................

**Closing and Prayer:** *Lord, thank You for delivering me from all fear even before I experience it. Thank You for eliminating all fear when you died for us on the cross. There is no reason to fear anything, because You are the sovereign God. Lord, please keep me guided on the right path, it's so easy for me to get lost in the day-to-day mundane, and it's so easy for fear to slip in. Fear of failure, fear of disappointment, fear of rejection, fear of the unknown; it's so easy to believe the lies the devil plants in my mind. Lord, I am always reminded of Your power and the fear that comes from knowing how sovereign You truly are. Remind me to fear You, the one who made me, and not the devil, who holds no legitimacy. Because of my faith in You, I have no reason to fear the devil. Amen.*

# CHAPTER SEVEN
## DO YOUR BEST

SCRIPTURE:

*"Whatever your hand finds to do, do it with all your might, for in the grave, where you are going, there is neither working nor planning nor knowledge nor wisdom."*

~ Ecclesiastes 9:10

SUMMARY:

Often times people think that success equates to a hefty amount of money in their bank account. To some, that is how they measure success, which is honestly sad. As Christian, we know that success isn't about dollar signs, but about the content of our character, and the effect this has on others. A large part of one's character is their work ethic and how hardworking you are. God instructs us to work to the best of our abilities, and to demonstrate His love in all that we do. All that we do is representative of our character, which is also a representation of Christ. To have poor work ethic would not be following Christ's commandments for us, and would set a bad example for non-believers. No matter your profession, no matter what you are doing, do it as if you are working directly for the Lord. Life is not about simply completing what you want to complete, it's about working to the best of your ability. The bible specifically outlines that with hard work comes great reward, while poverty comes with laziness. Look to those that are successful in your life, they are not that way because they took the easy way out. Most of the time it is because they dedicated their lives to their practice, and they emulate strong work ethic in all that they do. Follow God's instructions for your work ethic, and you will be honoring Him. Remember to do all things for His glory, and not for your own self-glory. He will reward those that do their work as unto Him.

POINTS TO REMEMBER:

- ❖ Success is measured by the strength of one's character, not by the amount of zero's in one's bank account.

- ❖ Christ instructs us to work to the best of our abilities, to use the gifts that He has bestowed upon each of us.

- ❖ When you are completing your job, are you doing it as if the service is for Jesus? Or would you change how you do it to make it better for Him? Do the same job for everyone that you would do for the Lord.

- ❖ The Lord will bless those that work hard.

- ❖ No matter what you are doing, do it for God's glory and not your own.

QUESTION & ANSWER:

*End of Chapter Questions to Consider:*

- ❖ Do you challenge yourself to do your best in all things?

- ❖ How do you react to obstacles?

- ❖ Do you or will you expect more than agreed-upon pay for a job well done?

- Are you a quitter, or do you have what it takes to achieve success in your life?

*End of Chapter Questions to Research:*

- Who is Samuel Truett Cathy?
- To what and whom does he attribute his success?

DO YOU HAVE ANY QUESTIONS? WRITE THEM HERE:

..................................................................................................................

..................................................................................................................

..................................................................................................................

..................................................................................................................

..................................................................................................................

..................................................................................................................

..................................................................................................................

SCRIPTURE VERSES TO MEMORIZE:

*"Lazy hands make a man poor, but diligent hands bring wealth."*
~ Proverbs 10:4

*"All hard work brings a profit, but mere talk only leads to poverty."*
~ Proverbs 14:23

JOURNAL YOUR THOUGHTS, WHAT DID YOU GAIN AND LEARN FROM THIS STUDY:

..................................................................................................

..................................................................................................

..................................................................................................

..................................................................................................

..................................................................................................

..................................................................................................

..................................................................................................

..................................................................................................

..................................................................................................

**Closing and Prayer:** *Dear Lord, I pray that You will direct my thoughts, and my actions towards You. In all that I do I want to honor You and praise Your name. I want to glorify You, and not myself. Thank You for giving me the determination each day to work to the best of my ability. Please Lord, never allow me to lose sight of what and who is important. That Your love reigns over all, and is supreme to all other things in life. Remind me to attribute all my success to You, as I couldn't do any of it without your strength, guidance or Your help. You are my very breath. Amen.*

# CHAPTER EIGHT
## TWO KINDS OF ANGER

SCRIPTURE:

*"A fool gives full vent to his anger, but a wise man keeps himself under control."*

~ Proverbs 29:11

SUMMARY:

The Bible articulates throughout that there are two types of anger, justified and unjustified. The emotion of justified anger is actually a natural born emotion that comes from God. Throughout the Bible we find Jesus living a sinless life on Earth, meanwhile showing the emotion of justified anger, occasionally. In John 2:13, Jesus became extremely angry when He entered a temple to find it being misused as a marketplace. He became furious at this sight, and drove all within, out of the temple. Jesus exemplifies justified anger, as there was a sinful activity taking place within His father's house.

Jesus is not the only person who can feel justified anger, as we all experience this. Justified anger can even be the force behind individuals who have brought about great change in history. Abraham Lincoln, signed the Proclamation Emancipation in 1863, where his justified anger over slavery brought about this change. It is important to learn how to deal with emotions, such as anger, so that the feelings are not harbored in a negative way. Anger can consume your mind, just as cancer consumes the body. Anger lacking purpose, is unjustified, and it is a sin. It is important to learn what makes you mad, what small things tend to aggravate you more than others. Once you can see these things in your own life, next you must learn to combat the negative reactions that come from these emotions.

The Bible warns of being quick to anger, and the foolishness it brings to a person. Even though we can work on our own personal anger, often times it is hard to deal with others that purposely say or do hurtful things to provoke an anger filled reaction. There are people who love to stir up dissension, who thrive off confrontation; you will have to learn to deal with these people throughout your life. Uncontrolled anger can lead to life changing or altering decisions that you will come to regret. These negative emotions can lead to heavy mistakes that cannot be taken back, mistakes that can lead to long-term damaging after effects. When someone confronts you in a confrontational way, learn to respond in a calmer, and peaceful manner. Sometimes the best thing one can do is simply not respond to confrontation, to let it die out on its own. Walk away from your pride, and allow their anger to be directed elsewhere. If you are mad, consider offering a piece of advice, but don't offer an insult or a put down the person. If you struggle with uncontrolled anger, ask God for His help in teaching you self-control.

POINTS TO REMEMBER:

- ❖ There are two types of anger, justified and unjustified.
- ❖ The bible teaches of justified anger and the change that can come from executing it properly.
- ❖ When we are angry, learn to handle the situation correctly, so that you can execute, and move on.
- ❖ Anger without cause is a sin.

- Life is full of irritations, learn to handle these emotions, and not allow trivial things to steal your peace or ultimately ruin your day.
- Learning to maintain self-control in every situation is crucial, it will help you avoid bad relations.

QUESTION & ANSWER:

*End of Chapter Questions to Consider:*

- When you become angry, is it usually justified or unjustified?
- How do you act when you're angry?
- What will you do and how will you react the next time you feel yourself becoming angry?

*End of Chapter Questions to Research:*

- Who is Dr. Benjamin Carson?
- How did he overcome uncontrolled anger in his life?
- How has God used his life to bless others?

DO YOU HAVE ANY QUESTIONS? WRITE THEM HERE:

..............................................................................................................

..............................................................................................................

..............................................................................................................

..............................................................................................................

..............................................................................................................

..............................................................................................................

..............................................................................................................

..............................................................................................................

..............................................................................................................

..............................................................................................................

SCRIPTURE VERSES TO MEMORIZE:

*"A gentle answer turns away wrath, but a harsh word stirs up anger."*
~ Proverbs 15:1

*"Do not be quickly provoked in your spirit, for anger resides in the laps of fools."*
~ Ecclesiastes 7:9

JOURNAL YOUR THOUGHTS, WHAT DID YOU GAIN AND LEARN FROM THIS STUDY:

..............................................................................................

..............................................................................................

..............................................................................................

..............................................................................................

..............................................................................................

..............................................................................................

..............................................................................................

..............................................................................................

..............................................................................................

..............................................................................................

**Closing and Prayer:** *Dear Lord, Today I come to You thanking You for the emotions that You gave to us. I am thankful that I can feel happy when I do well, that I can feel sad when I miss a friend, or that I can feel surprised. Lord, I am also thankful for the feeling of justified anger. I am grateful for this emotion, but I need help controlling it so it does not turn into unjustified anger. Teach me to be slow to anger, and wise in my words. Thank You for your constant guidance Jesus, Amen.*

# CHAPTER NINE
# FORGIVE EVERYTHING?

SCRIPTURE:

*"If you forgive men when they sin against you, your heavenly Father will also forgive you. But, if you do not forgive men their sins, your Father will not forgive your sins."*

~ Matthew 6:14–15

SUMMARY:

As Christians, we believe that we are all sinners. The only sinless man to ever walk earth was Jesus Christ. Throughout time we will be affected by our own sin, but also that of others. Over time we will be hurt by others, whether it is intentional or unintentional, but the one thing we will all have to do is to learn how to forgive. God puts people into our lives for many different reasons. Some people are for friendship, some are for relationships, others are simply passing by. Sometimes people come into our lives that we may not necessarily understand. Sometimes God purposely puts people in our lives in order to help mold our character into who He wants us to be. Whatever the case, or whatever the purpose, things in life happen for a reason, even though we might not always understand it. Different from this, forgiveness makes complete sense.

Although God commands us to forgive all wrongs committed against us, He does not command us to stay close to friends who may have committed wrongs against us. Although there is purpose in each encounter, it does not mean we must have lifelong relationships with all those we encounter. We must understand that forgiveness and trust are two different things. Sometimes when a person offends you, the relationship can be restored and strengthened; and this is important in covenant relationships like marriage. Other times, it cannot. God wants us to forgive, but He does not expect us to continue to foster a relationship that may be toxic. One hard, but important lesson that we must learn throughout our lives is letting those who walk away from us, walk away. If the person is meant to be a part of your future, then they will return, but if not, let it be.

Not only will others hurt us throughout our lives, but we will also hurt others. Because of this, we will have to learn to forgive ourselves, as God forgives us. Once we invite the Holy Spirit into our lives, asking Him to take the lead, we will become increasingly closer to God. We must understand that we will still mess up from time to time, even if our faith in God is strong. You might even struggle more with forgiving yourself over forgiving others. Understand that God loved us first, so that we could love others. If we truly love others, then we will know how to forgive others. The business of forgiving is not just for those that we love, though. We must forgive all, even those that we do not like. We must leave judgement up to God, while making it right with the person. Forgiveness, although much about the other person, is very much about ourselves. Forgiving someone brings freedom for us, while harboring hurt feelings only worsens things for us. There is a purpose in all things, so that harboring hurt feelings over something is just ignoring the possible point in an event. God repays those without remorse, and He forgives those with remorse for wrongs committed against another. Forgive yourself.

POINTS TO REMEMBER:

- ❖ All humans are sinners.

- ❖ Due to our sinful nature, we will do things to hurt others, as the same will be done to us. We will be hurt by those close to us, and we must learn how to forgive others of their wrongful acts.

- ❖ Learning to forgive is hard, but absolutely necessary for our own good.

- ❖ God puts people into our lives for many different reasons, reasons we might not recognize until much later.

- ❖ God commands us to forgive all wrongs committed against us, but does not command us to keep toxic relationships in our lives.

- ❖ Sometimes people walk away from us because of a reason, which is unseen, but we need to let them go. If it is meant to be they will return.

- ❖ Forgiveness goes both ways. Not only do we need to learn how to forgive others, but we must know how to forgive ourselves when we mess up.

- ❖ Without forgiveness, it would be impossible to maintain relationships.

- ❖ Forgiving someone brings freedom for us, while harboring hurt feelings only worsens things for us.

QUESTION & ANSWER:

Do you struggle with forgiveness? Do you recognize that forgiveness is something you must give yourself, as well as others? Do you struggle with forgiving yourself more than you struggle with forgiving others?

*End of Chapter Questions to Consider:*

- ❖ Do you struggle with forgiving others?
- ❖ How long does it take you to forgive?
- ❖ Do you want others to forgive you when you mess up?
- ❖ Do you need to forgive yourself for something?

DO YOU HAVE ANY QUESTIONS? WRITE THEM HERE:

..............................................................................................................

..............................................................................................................

..............................................................................................................

..............................................................................................................

..............................................................................................................

..............................................................................................................

..............................................................................................................

SCRIPTURE VERSES TO MEMORIZE:

> *"For all have sinned and fall short of the glory of God."*
> ~ Romans 3:23

> *"Do not seek revenge, or bear grudge against anyone among your people, but love your neighbor as yourself. I am the Lord."*
> ~ Leviticus 19:18

JOURNAL YOUR THOUGHTS, WHAT DID YOU GAIN AND LEARN FROM THIS STUDY:

..................................................................................................

..................................................................................................

..................................................................................................

..................................................................................................

..................................................................................................

..................................................................................................

..................................................................................................

..................................................................................................

**Closing and Prayer:** *Dear Lord, Thank You for teaching us about forgiveness through your actions. Thank You for giving us the ultimate example found in Your Son and His sacrificial life. Thank You for forgiving us of our sins on the cross, even before we commit them. Jesus, we want to thank You for Your gift of forgiveness, and allowing us to forgive others. Thank You for teaching us to forgive others, but to also forgive ourselves as well. Please teach me to forgive myself when I mess up, as well as forgiving others when they mess up as well. Amen.*

# CHAPTER TEN
# YOUR GREATEST FANS

SCRIPTURE:

*"Listen, my son, to your father's instruction and do not forsake your mother's teaching."*

~ Proverbs 1:8

SUMMARY:

The fifth commandment listed in the ten commandments is to honor your father and mother. The Bible is ever clear that we must honor our father and mothers. Parents are given the responsibility of preparing children for adulthood, by teaching each child to be a respectful and resourceful human being. Often times children get annoyed at their parents because they set up rules for them, but they are simply doing their God-ordained job. In fact, there is no greater human love than the love a parent has for a child. Most parents will tell others that they will not understand love until they experience the love for a child. Not only is the love connection between a parent and child the greatest in the world, but the commitment, sacrifice, and work involved in raising a child is the greatest responsibility God has given to a person.

Being a parent isn't an easy job. You must care for your child round the clock, and when they are infants is most hours of the day. You must be completely self-less, giving up not only your money, but your time, as well as your individualism. As you grow up you will start to understand more and more how much responsibility God bestows upon parents. Parents must provide for their children, while children simply just have to give them the respect that the Bible talks about. Throughout their lives parents will experience things that shape their knowledge of the world and those experiences will trickle into how they parent and bring their children up. It is the job of parents to teach children right from wrong, but to also teach them the wrongs of the world. Not only should you respect your parents, but you should bring joy to them by obeying them.

POINTS TO REMEMBER:

- The Fifth commandment is to honor your father and mother.

- Parenthood brings great responsibility, and is a selfless task. It is one to be respected, as God instructs us.

- There is no greater human love than the love a parent has for their child.

- Not only is the love connection between a parent and child the greatest in the world, the commitment, sacrifice, and work involved in raising a child is the most awesome responsibility God gives to anyone.

- Parents dedicate their lives to doing the very best they can to ensure their children have everything they need to succeed in life.

- Upon birth, the parent's role moves to second, as the child's life and needs become priority.

- Parents possess wisdom that you will not know as a child, until you experience as much as they have.

- When we do something wrong, there are often consequences that follow. Parents or parental figures will teach us this basic principle as they will be the first to execute this in children's lives.

- It's not only your parents' job to teach you right from wrong and how to live, but it's also their job to do their very best to protect you from the evils of the world until you reach the age where you can make proper decisions and take care of yourself.

- Always adhere to your parent's guidance and instruction.

- The Bible not only commands us to honor our parents, but also to bring joy to our parents. You can do this by simply respecting them.

QUESTION & ANSWER:

Do you understand the importance of obeying your mother and father? Do you find this commandment to be harder or easier for you to obey? Is this something that you need to work on? If so, what can you do to change this behavior?

*End of Chapter Questions to Consider:*

- How do you currently view your parents?

- What are some sacrifices your parents have made for you?

- How do you show them respect?

- What is the greatest gift you can give your parents?

DO YOU HAVE ANY QUESTIONS? WRITE THEM HERE:

........................................................................................................

........................................................................................................

........................................................................................................

........................................................................................................

........................................................................................................

........................................................................................................

........................................................................................................

........................................................................................................

........................................................................................................

........................................................................................................

SCRIPTURE VERSES TO MEMORIZE:

> *"Honor your father and your mother, so that you may live long in the land the Lord your God is giving you."*
>
> ~ Exodus 20:12

> *"A wise son brings joy to his father, but a foolish son grief to his mother."*
>
> ~ Proverbs 10:1

JOURNAL YOUR THOUGHTS, WHAT DID YOU GAIN AND LEARN FROM THIS STUDY:

..................................................................................................................

..................................................................................................................

..................................................................................................................

..................................................................................................................

..................................................................................................................

..................................................................................................................

..................................................................................................................

..................................................................................................................

..................................................................................................................

..................................................................................................................

**Closing and Prayer:** *Dear Lord, Thank You for providing me with parents, or parental figures, who look out for my best intentions. Thank you for being the greatest Father to us, and an example of love to all parents out there. Lord, thank You for being in control of our lives, and teaching us to obey our parents. Please give me patience and guidance in obeying and respecting my parents. Amen.*

# CHAPTER ELEVEN
# LOVING OTHERS

SCRIPTURE:

*The commandments, "Do not commit adultery," "Do not murder," "Do not steal," "Do not covet," and whatever other commandment there may be, are summed up in this one rule: "Love your neighbor as yourself." Love does no harm to its neighbor. Therefore, love is the fulfillment of the law."*

~ Romans 13:9–10

SUMMARY:

Throughout the Bible, God outlines many commandments, as well as promises He has for us. He has guidelines and commandments for us because of His immense love for us, while promising us a variety of things throughout scripture. One of His greatest promises in scripture is the promise of His unconditional love, for He sent His son to die for our sins. In 1st Corinthians 13, Jesus tells us that the greatest commandment of all is to love Him, and then to love others. To truly love another, we must serve one another.

God calls us to love everyone, but as explained in the previous chapter, not everyone that you come across is meant to be a close friend. Surround yourself with like-minded Christians who also made the decision to abandon human nature, and follow Christ. It is important to note that the Bible does not tell you to treat others as they treat you, but to treat them how you want to be treated. It's very easy to slip into the train of thought that you should treat others the way they treat you, but that simply is not true. Regardless of what is done to you, it is important to remember what the Bible says. Christ does not treat us the way we treat Him, or we would have a much different relationship with God. Often times it is hard to show the love of God when someone is making you mad. Learn to ignore negative comments, conduct yourself as the bigger person, leaving no space to entertain foolishness. It is also important to not waste your time worried about whether or not someone likes you. If you are striving to be the best you can be and your heart is in the right place, then simply understand that not everyone will like you, for various reasons. This does not give you an excuse to ignore God's commandment, and not show love to others, this is something that should be consistent in your life. Being this kind of person, demonstrates God's love, and sets an example for those around you.

Aside from treating others with the upmost respect, as Christians, we are also called to give to those who are less fortunate than we are. You can give money, or material possessions, but also can give your time. Giving to others not only blesses them, but it will bless your soul as well. Having a genuine love for God's people is important and will allow you to be an example to others. Things like race, ethnicity, gender, etc. can lead to prejudice, but this is not what God wants. You are to love others equally, with the same love God loves you with. A few kind words, or kind acts go a long way and it is an easy way to show others how you love them.

POINTS TO REMEMBER:

- ❖ The Bible tells us that the greatest commandment is to love God, the second greatest is to love others.

- ❖ To truly love another, we must serve one another.

- ❖ To serve another is to support and sympathize in the greatest capacity.

- ❖ "Do unto others as you would have them do unto you" rings true always

- ❖ Sometimes it is hard to remember the importance of ALWAYS demonstrating the Lord's love when people are hateful.

- ❖ Do not entertain foolishness, be the bigger person in all situations.

- ❖ Not every person that comes across your path will like you, come to peace with this.

- ❖ Giving will bless others, as well as bless yourself.

- ❖ Be a light to others: every facial expression, every act, and every word that comes out of your mouth matters.

- ❖ When loving others, they will see it and it will return.

- ❖ Never do anything in malice.

- ❖ Be kind to everyone.

QUESTION & ANSWER:

Do you know what the greatest commandment is according to Jesus? Do you follow this commandment? Or do you find it hard to follow this commandment?

*End of Chapter Questions to Consider:*

- ❖ What would you have done if you were the Samaritan traveling along the road that day?
- ❖ Do you always strive to do what is right in the eyes of God?
- ❖ What changes do you need to make in your thinking and in your life with regard to loving others?
- ❖ Do you ever acknowledge strangers?

DO YOU HAVE ANY QUESTIONS? WRITE THEM HERE:

..........................................................................................................................................

..........................................................................................................................................

..........................................................................................................................................

..........................................................................................................................................

..........................................................................................................................................

SCRIPTURE VERSES TO MEMORIZE:

*"So in everything, do to others what you would have them do to you, for this sums up the Law and the Prophets."*
~ Matthew 7:12

*"Flee the evil desires of youth, and pursue righteousness, faith, love and peace, along with those who call on the Lord out of a pure heart."* 2
~ Timothy 2:22

JOURNAL YOUR THOUGHTS, WHAT DID YOU GAIN AND LEARN FROM THIS STUDY:

..............................................................................................................................

..............................................................................................................................

..............................................................................................................................

..............................................................................................................................

..............................................................................................................................

..............................................................................................................................

..............................................................................................................................

..............................................................................................................................

..............................................................................................................................

**Closing and Prayer:** *Dear Lord, thank You for giving us the Bible to instruct us on how to live. I appreciate that You specifically outline rights form wrong, and blessings from curses. Thank You for loving us first, so that we could then love others. Thank You for showering us with the ultimate love, so that we could then shower others with love. Thank You for being the greatest example of love, and the greatest example of showing us what it is like to love in a wholly selfless way. Thank You for giving us the ability to love, and the ability to lean on You for this love. God, guide me, instruct me, teach me. Teach me to love more like You. An unconditional and all-encompassing love. Thank You, Jesus, Amen.*

# CHAPTER TWELVE
# NO ROOM FOR ENVY

SCRIPTURE:

*"Each one should test his own actions. Then he can take pride in himself, without comparing himself to somebody else, for each one should carry his own load."*

~ Galatians 6:4–5

SUMMARY:

Since the beginning of time, envy has been the cause of much disorder in the world, and often times being at the root of sin. The feeling of envy can drive people to do terrible things, as we see this demonstrated in the Bible on a few different occasions. We see this in Genesis 4, with Cain and Abel, and again in Genesis 37 with the story of Joseph and his brothers. Both stories demonstrate discord in families that is a result of feelings of envy. Do not worry about what others have, or what others are doing. Focus on your life, and your accomplishments, as they are just as important as anyone else's. God commands us to be mindful of one another, but to mind our own business, while being thankful for our blessings.

You will never be able to enjoy peace in your heart if you are always focused on others and their lives. If you are only focused on keeping up with others, or out-doing others, you will miss the plan God has for you, and your life. Often times, you will find yourself idolizing others, and what they do. This is a sin, as you are worshipping something that is not the Lord. Everyone is different, and there is a different plan for each and every person.

Those who knowingly do wrong to others don't live in peace, because they know they're not living right. They also are constantly looking over their shoulders, trying to keep others from finding out what they are doing. God will bless those that live according to His will. Keep in mind that others may be envious of you, and will try to attack you for certain things. Seek God in these situations and He will guide you in His wisdom.

POINTS TO REMEMBER:

- Envy is discontent and resentment over others. Envy is a sin.
- The feeling of envy is so powerful that it can cause people to make poor decisions, or do bad things.
- Envy is foolishness, as it is a waste of time for those that entertain it.
- Rejoice in the attributes and successes of others, as you want others to do for you.
- Keep God at the forefront of your mind at all times, there will be no room for envy or disdain of others.
- When you have a relationship with God, stand up for what is right as you will constantly be targeted from others.
- Love looks past faults, hate exploits them.
- Envy is wicked, and it will get the best of those that do not see themselves as God sees them.
- When others strike at you due to envy, just ignore them and pray for their insecurities to be healed.

QUESTION & ANSWER:

Do you struggle with envy? Do you often find yourself jealous of others, whether it's their appearance or different aspects of their lives? Do you understand the uniqueness each person has because of Gods intentionality in creating each person differently? What can you do to curb your envy when it arises?

*End of Chapter Questions to Consider:*

- ❖ Is there someone you envy? If so, how do you intend to change?
- ❖ How do you recognize a hater?
- ❖ How did Jesus deal with His haters?
- ❖ How will you deal with yours in the future?

DO YOU HAVE ANY QUESTIONS? WRITE THEM HERE:

....................................................................................................................................

....................................................................................................................................

....................................................................................................................................

....................................................................................................................................

....................................................................................................................................

....................................................................................................................................

....................................................................................................................................

....................................................................................................................................

SCRIPTURE VERSES TO MEMORIZE:

*"And I saw that all labor and all achievement spring from man's envy of his neighbor. This too is meaningless, a chasing after the wind."*
~ Ecclesiastes 4:4

*"Do not let your heart envy sinners, but always be zealous for the fear of the Lord.*
*There is surely a future hope for you, and your hope will not be cut off."*
~ Proverbs 23:17–18

JOURNAL YOUR THOUGHTS, WHAT DID YOU GAIN AND LEARN FROM THIS STUDY:

..................................................................................................

..................................................................................................

..................................................................................................

..................................................................................................

..................................................................................................

..................................................................................................

..................................................................................................

..................................................................................................

..................................................................................................

..................................................................................................

**Closing and Prayer:** *Dear Lord, Today I want to thank You for always being there for us. I want to thank You for creating each and every one of us in a unique way. Thank You for doing this with purpose, so that every person would be different. I am so grateful for Your kindness and Your grace. God give me the grace and kindness to deal with others who are envious of me. Give me the strength to not feel envious of others. I am so thankful that You are always there to help me through my struggles, and guide me away from negatives like envy, and always towards truth. Amen.*

# CHAPTER THIRTEEN
# HOW SERIOUS IS GOSSIP?

SCRIPTURE:

*Jesus called the crowd to him and said, "Listen and understand. What goes into a man's mouth does not make him 'unclean,' but what comes out of his mouth, that is what makes him 'unclean.'"*

~ Matthew 15:10–11

SUMMARY:

Throughout this book we learned who you are as an individual, and the power of God that we possess within us. In chapter thirteen, the topic of gossip is discussed. Throughout the Bible, we watch as God ridicules gossip, even hates it. Gossip is defined as "the repeat of chatter or idle talk and rumors, especially about the private affairs of others." Similar to envy, which was discussed in the previous chapter, people everywhere gossip. It is rare to find people that do not gossip casually amidst conversation. It seems to be hard for people to keep things confidential these days. It is important, when telling someone something in confidentiality, that you trust that they will not tell someone else. Even if it is unintentional, it is still wrong to share something that someone asked you to keep private.

Learn to be someone that can keep things confidential. When someone tells you something, make sure the person is telling you, and not anyone else. It is a good practice to learn to keep another's business out of casual conversation. Gossip is not only restricted to telling ones secret's, it is also discussing others private business. Most of the time this business is not positive either. Usually if it is being discussed it is something bad that surrounds another human being. It does not matter how juicy a story might be, it still is not your place to talk about it. Gossip can be extremely hurtful, and is also seldom accurate. Use the self-control that God gave you, and control the things that come out of your mouth. Even when someone says or does something to hurt your feelings, do not retaliate. People will gossip about you, and some of the time you will find out. Other times you won't, but the overarching point is to demonstrate self-control and do not react in a malicious manner. Gossip is never justified, but neither is a negative reaction. Turn away from the practice of gossip, and focus on the positive things in life.

POINTS TO REMEMBER:

- God hates gossip, the Bible specifically warns against it.
- Similar to envy, you will find people gossiping just about everywhere you go.
- Rise above, and be the bigger person. Do not gossip, for it is a sin.
- Be someone that can keep things confidential, more people will trust you, and friendships will strengthen because of it.
- A good practice is to ignore gossip, and start new conversational topics when it is brought into conversation.
- Another good practice is to only say positive things about others, that way negative gossip can be completely eradicated.
- Like the golden rule states, "Treat others the way you want to be treated," and do not gossip about others.

QUESTION & ANSWER:

Do you often times find yourself filling awkward silences with gossip? When you are bored, or do not know what to talk about do you turn to gossip? If you do not struggle with gossip, what techniques have you used to rid yourself of it?

*Questions to Consider:*

- ❖ Why does gossip infuriate God?
- ❖ What changes do you need to make in your life regarding gossip?
- ❖ How will you respond the next time someone comes to you with gossip?
- ❖ How will you respond the next time you learn someone has gossiped about you?

DO YOU HAVE ANY QUESTIONS? WRITE THEM HERE:

...................................................................................................................

...................................................................................................................

...................................................................................................................

...................................................................................................................

...................................................................................................................

...................................................................................................................

...................................................................................................................

SCRIPTURE VERSES TO MEMORIZE:

*"A gossip betrays a confidence, but a trustworthy man keeps a secret."*
~ Proverbs 11:13

*"A prudent man keeps his knowledge to himself, but the heart of fools blurts out folly."*
~ Proverbs 12:23

JOURNAL YOUR THOUGHTS, WHAT DID YOU GAIN AND LEARN FROM THIS STUDY:

..................................................................................................

..................................................................................................

..................................................................................................

..................................................................................................

..................................................................................................

..................................................................................................

..................................................................................................

**Closing and Prayer:** *Dear Lord, thank You for giving me the ability to talk, and converse with other people. Thank You for allowing us freedom of speech. Lord, please guide my mouth, and give me the strength to not talk about others. Thank You for loving me even though I do mess up, and helping me back up when I need it. Amen.*

# CHAPTER FOURTEEN
# HOW ABOUT A LITTLE WHITE LIE?

SCRIPTURE:

*"The wisdom of the prudent is to give thought to their ways, but the folly of fools is deception."*

~ Proverbs 14:8

SUMMARY:

From the time we are little we are told that lying is wrong. Throughout the Bible there are seven things that God hates. This includes lying. It does not matter your intentions; a lie is a lie and it is wrong. Some people think that it is okay to lie in order to avoid hurting someone's feelings, but these "white lies" are actually wrong as well. Simple things like saying your honest opinion when asked, or saying no to a date you do not want to go on, are important things. The Bible reiterates time-after-time the importance of telling the truth, even when it is hard. Truthfulness is a quality that comes with someone who is also trustworthy. If someone can be honest, and tell you the truth, then they are also, most likely, a trustworthy person.

On the other side, there are people who constantly lie, and say things in order to either help themselves, or help another person. Typically, if someone is constantly lying about things, they are probably not the most trustworthy person. In the Bible, it is explained that God hates lying. He holds disdain for the sin, and commands us not to lie. Furthermore, we should especially not tell a lie about another human. That is a slander. If you engage in slanderous statements, you should not worry as much about the person finding out what you said, but about God holding you accountable. Lying can also be a downward spiral, just like all sins can be. It is human nature to mess up every occasionally, as we are all sinful beings, but that does not give you an excuse for poor behavior. You possess the power to control your mouth, and with God's help you can live a life free of lies.

POINTS TO REMEMBER:

- All lies are lies, even small white lies.
- The Bible explicitly details that lying is a sin, and something that God hates.
- Even when you are trying to avoid hurting another's feelings, white lies are not appropriate.
- Sometimes in telling the truth, people will be hurt, but you need to learn to be truthful, in the kindest way possible.
- People who are truthful, are usually very trustworthy as well.
- People who lie more, tend to be less trustworthy, and not someone you would want to tell important things to.
- Finding people to trust is important so you can confide in a few, trustworthy individuals.
- When someone has a problem with white lies, it is easy for them to fall down a slippery slope where lying becomes second nature.

QUESTION & ANSWER:

Have you ever found yourself caught in a lie? More so have you ever found yourself caught spreading a lie about another person? It is easy to tell white lies and think that they are okay because of the smallness of them, but all lies are lies. If you have a problem with lying ask God for guidance, and find an accountability partner to help you through this sin.

*End of Chapter Questions to Consider:*

- ❖ Why does God hate lying so much?
- ❖ Where do you stand with God regarding lying?
- ❖ How do you react when you discover someone has lied about you?

DO YOU HAVE ANY QUESTIONS? WRITE THEM HERE:

........................................................................................................................................

........................................................................................................................................

........................................................................................................................................

........................................................................................................................................

........................................................................................................................................

........................................................................................................................................

........................................................................................................................................

........................................................................................................................................

........................................................................................................................................

SCRIPTURE VERSES TO MEMORIZE:

*"The Lord detests lying lips, but He delights in men who are truthful."*
~ Proverbs 12:22

*"Remove from me the way of lying; and grant me thy law graciously."*
~ Psalm 119:29

JOURNAL YOUR THOUGHTS, WHAT DID YOU GAIN AND LEARN FROM THIS STUDY:

........................................................................................................

........................................................................................................

........................................................................................................

........................................................................................................

........................................................................................................

........................................................................................................

**Closing and Prayer:** *Dear Lord, Thank You for giving us the ability to talk and speak with freedom. I pray that You will help me to always speak truth, and not to lie, even in a small way, I understand that white lies can lead down a destructive path and that is a sinful behavior. Help me to keep my words not only pure, but true. Lord, keep me from gossiping, and always speaking kindly of others. Thank You for giving me the freedom to speak my mind, but help me harness it in a way that praises You. Amen.*

www.ingramcontent.com/pod-product-compliance
Lightning Source LLC
Chambersburg PA
CBHW081348040426
42450CB00015B/3352